Dahlias for Cut Flowe

The Hay Lane Grower's Handbook Vol 2

J. Hutcheon and J.F. Hutcheon

Introduction

No artisan cut flower farm is complete without a bed of dahlias. Always in demand from florists and beloved by the almost everyone these showy and beautiful flowers are the essential late summer bloom.

Dahlias originated in semi-tropical parts of Mexico and are named for the Swedish botanist Anders Dahl. Dahl originally imported them as a possible food source for their edible tubers. Dahlia plants were first imported into Europe in 1791 and we've been hybridising and selecting ever since.

Available to grow in such a huge range of colours and forms, it is almost impossible to choose which varieties to concentrate on. And they are not easy to grow so buying varieties that will do well is important. As a cut flower they do not travel well, being delicate and difficult to transport. The flowers do not open if cut in bud, so their vase life is limited. This makes it very tricky for the large-scale overseas flower growers to get them to market in good condition. So, the best place, by far, for florists and flower lovers to buy good quality dahlias from is their local cut flower grower.

To compete with run of the mill, lack-lustre imported blooms that do make it to the large wholesale markets it is vital that small scale growers offer only the highest quality blooms that command a high stem price. Dahlias are expensive and time-consuming to grow and so it is worth taking the time to learn how to do it well. And to that end if you really want to grow a perfect dahlia, please, please, please join the National Dahlia Society. The amateur growers who spend a large proportion of their lives chasing exhibition bench gold medals know more about growing dahlias than most of us ever will.

Jane

Contents

Buying dahlias

Dahlias are sold as tubers during the winter and spring, as plants during the spring (rooted cuttings or mini plants) and in summer as garden ready potted plants.

Tubers will give you a larger plant in the first year, and most usefully the opportunity to start them into growth early in the year so that many cuttings may be taken from new growth. However, if tubers are sourced from anywhere but a reputable supplier you run the risk of receiving plants which are the wrong variety, poor quality or even worse carrying disease.

Pot tubers a pot tuber is a smaller tuber, grown in a pot to restrict its size. It is a particularly useful way to create manageable sized tubers from varieties that normally grow very large over the course of one season and works well to help improve survival rates of varieties that usually struggle to make good tubers. Where post and packing and limited propagation space are issues, using pot tubers for providing cutting material is a very good solution.

Rooted cuttings or mini plants are a cheaper option than tubers. The plant you receive will be a small plant with good root growth and at least two pairs of leaves. It may well have been 'stopped' – had the growing tip pinched out, to stop the plant getting too tall and promote bushy growth. They will not yet have a tuber but will make a good-sized one over the coming growing season, which will be suitable for storing over the next winter. If you order rooted cuttings early in the year, you must be sure you have a heated space to grow them on in. If ordered early enough it is possible to take cuttings from these small plants to increase your stock. Many people worry that these small plants will not make enough growth to be productive flower producers in their first year. This is not the case and most professional growers and exhibitors prefer to grow their stock new from cuttings every year as it usually gives better-quality blooms. Over time old tubers become more likely to become diseased or weakened, so it really does make sense to learn how to take cuttings to keep your stock fresh and healthy.

<u>Garden ready plants</u> are an expensive way to buy dahlias and of little use to the grower, the sale of these plants is aimed more at gardeners.

<u>Seed</u>

Unfortunately, dahlias do not come true from seed. Cheap seed sold online may seem like a quick way to get lots of plants, however the plants you grow will be variable, often with single flowers and almost always of no value as a cut flower. You may be able to purchase seed directly from a reputable dahlia breeder, which has resulted from careful cross pollination between good dahlia varieties. Although the chances of getting a good quality bloom from these plants is now somewhat higher, it is still not a certainty, and you will need to raise every seedling to flowering size before you will find out if you have anything worth keeping or not. And you can always try your own hand at seed saving to see what you get. Growing dahlias from saved seed is a fun activity as you never know what you will get, but the chances of getting a plant good enough to be worth keeping are slim at best.

Seed should be sown six weeks before your last frost date. Pre-germinating seeds on damp paper towels means only the viable seeds are potted up. Germination should occur within ten days. The seeds can then be potted up for growing on into small pots, which should be grown on in a warm place with good light. If light levels are too low, seedlings will quickly become leggy.

Dahlia suppliers

The importance of buying your plants or tubers from a reputable supplier cannot be emphasised enough, preferably one who grows their own stock. We have listed our favourite dahlia suppliers in the appendix.

Plants grown for the larger retail market in vast fields are harvested mechanically, with very little disease control. Tubers are damaged in the harvesting and packing process, and can often arrive desiccated, with a greatly reduced chance of sprouting or with broken necks or no crown, meaning there is no chance of them growing at all. Getting a mislabelled variety or a tuber with disease has become worryingly common when buying from these suppliers. It is very frustrating to buy a tuber, take cuttings from it, happily plant out your twenty beautiful cuttings only to find that you were sold the wrong variety and now have twenty yellow cactus dahlias, when you thought you would have twenty peach waterlily types. It is even worse to plant out a tuber and later find it is diseased and realise that you may have unwittingly infected your healthy plants and contaminated your soil.

Starting tubers for cuttings under cover

Tubers can of course be planted out where they are to flower as soon you are sure the last frost date is imminent. However, there are many reasons for starting tubers off earlier under cover, the main one being that you will then be able to take cuttings from the new growth early enough to get strong plants that will flower well in their first year.

If you are lucky enough to have a heated greenhouse or a bright heated conservatory you can start dahlia tubers for taking cuttings from as early as February (and some growers start even earlier). With the low light levels in February and March new growth can be leggy and weak, so we usually wait until March to start our tubers. The earlier you start the more space you will need for the growing tubers and their cuttings, which once well rooted will grow incredibly quickly. There is no point starting the tubers off too early if you do not have the space and time to look after, and pot on the cuttings. They will need to be kept in a heated, bright and airy environment until they can go out into the unheated greenhouse or polytunnel, for the gradual process of hardening off, in late spring.

Tubers can be potted up in individual pots or crates into regular potting compost. It is best practice to leave the crowns of the tubers exposed as this will make it easier to access the new shoots for taking cuttings later. Lightly water the tubers and site them in a warm area to sprout. Once new growth has started the tubers must be placed in a brightly lit area, natural sunlight is good, but grow lights may be used if needed. If new growth looks leggy it is an indicator that extra light is needed.

Your tubers will take anywhere from ten days upwards to start forming new shoots. How long it takes is dependent on growing conditions, variety and the condition of the tuber. New growth will start from the eyes, which are the small buds present on the crowns of the tubers. Broken pieces of tuber, which do not have a neck or part of the crown attached to them will not have eyes and hence will not grow.

Young shoots forming from 'eyes' on the crown of a dahlia tuber.

Taking cuttings from tubers

When your young shoots reach over 10 cm in length and have a good set of new leaves on them you will be able to start taking cuttings. With a sharp, clean knife slice the new shoot off, close to the base. Some growers take a small slice of the tuber with their cutting material, but we do not as it is unnecessary. The area where you cut the shoot from will soon dry up and multiple new eyes will form around the edges of the wound, which will give you even more cutting material in a couple of weeks' time.

If the base of your cutting looks clean you can start to root it straight away. If it does not you can trim it up or slice the shoot neatly, just below a node (as with any softwood cuttings).

If your shoot is excessively thick at the base or has a hollow stem already, it's chances of rooting are significantly lower. Some varieties, such as American Dawn, naturally throw out very chunky shoots. However, if you've already cut it, you might as well try to root it, as you've nothing to lose.

Tubers with lots of shoots suitable for cuttings.

It is important when taking cuttings to clean the knife you use regularly to minimise the chances of spreading any disease between plants. Pots or trays that are used to root the cuttings should also be reasonably clean.

Split node cuttings

If you are short of cutting material or really want to increase your stock of a variety quickly, you could always have a go at taking a few split node cuttings. Remove a medium thickness shoot from the tuber, pinch out it's tip above a node, and then split it lengthwise, with a sharp knife from base to the top between the nodes. Root each half of the cutting as if they were separate cuttings. It's a buy one, get one free kind of thing.

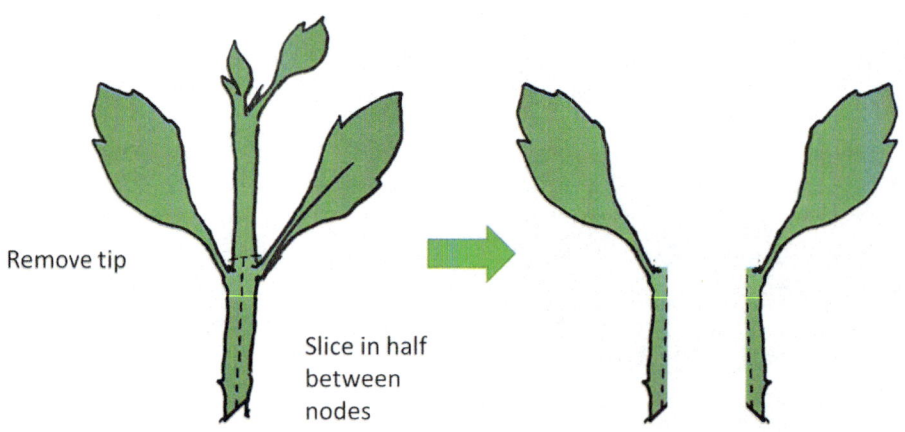

Remove tip

Slice in half between nodes

A split node cutting can produce two cuttings from one shoot.

Methods to root your cuttings

Into compost

Cuttings can be rooted into pots of potting compost mixed with vermiculite inside a clear plastic bag or propagator. If you are taking a lot of cuttings, you can use modules which fit into a propagator or tray. You can use hormone rooting powder or liquid to aid rooting if you would like to, but we do not as we find the cuttings usually root quite well without it.

Early in the year when it is still cool at night cuttings will root more readily with bottom heat. This could be inside a heated propagator or just by placing pots on a heat mat.

Cuttings rooted this way form strong roots and grow quickly once potted on.

Cuttings in potting compost, a clear plastic propagator lid will cover the cuttings to keep them hydrated until they root.

In a mist propagator

Mist propagators provide a very humid, controlled temperature environment where rooting takes place quickly. The cutting is suspended in a foam support within the propagator, above a water reservoir and water is continually sprayed at the base of the cutting. On warm days the propagator vents should be opened as sometimes the excessive humidity can cause the cutting material to rot, however the percentage of successful rooting is very high.

The propagators are expensive and need an electric supply to heat the water and run the pump. The new roots on the plants are weak and long and will need potting up quickly, and they do take longer to get going once potted up than the plants rooted directly into potting compost.

Cuttings ready to go in the mist propagator.

In a rock wool sheet

Rock wool can be used in place of potting compost. Sheets of rockwool blocks are readily available with premade holes for the cuttings from horticultural suppliers. Simply place the sheets onto a tray, water and allow the rock wool to absorb the water and insert your cutting material into the hole. Rooting is quick and the of percentage of successful rooting is usually good.

Rock wool cubes with dahlia cuttings

The cuttings in rock wool can be transplanted straight in to compost for growing on. Removing the cuttings from the rock wool without damaging them is tricky but can be done. Rock wool is not biodegradable and quite expensive. It also is produced in a process which is damaging to the environment. If you do choose to use it, try to reuse the blocks as many times as possible.

<u>In water</u>

Some people find they can root dahlia cuttings simply be placing the base of the stems in a glass of water on a windowsill. We've never had much success with this method.

<u>Factors which affect the rate of rooting</u>

Cuttings taken early in the season do not root as easily as those taken later, so do not automatically blame your technique if you have poor rooting rates in February. By mid-March, when the natural light is stronger, and the days are warmer the cuttings will root more quickly and be less likely to rot. Heat mats and grow lights can be used to create better growing conditions if desired.

If you have cuttings in a pot that are starting to turn black and rot, remove them quickly to prevent the rot from spreading.

Use of a hormone rooting powder or liquid early in the season will speed up the rooting process.

Some varieties are very easy to successfully take cuttings from, while others may have lots of lovely looking shoots that are very reluctant to root. I have never had a cutting of Aljo that did not root but struggle every year with rooting the cuttings of American Dawn. There is often no rhyme or reason to it.

Potting on and caring for your cuttings

Once their roots are established cuttings will grow quickly, they need good light and repotting regularly to prevent leggy or weak growth. When the cutting has formed at least three good sets of leaves the top of the cutting can be pinched out to promote bushy growth. When plants are big enough you can also take tip cuttings from them and increase your stock even more.

As you are growing your cuttings inside in a warm environment you will need to keep an eye out for pests such as aphids or spider mite (see section on problems, pests and diseases).

Cuttings taken in March can often be large enough to need potting into a 2L pot by May. Harden cuttings off gradually before planting out after the last frosts.

Cuttings need potting on regularly, and must be kept in a warm, well-lit area until it is mild enough to start the hardening off process.

Starting tubers indoors to get ahead

If you would like to start tubers off under cover just to get ahead and check that all of your tubers are viable before planting them out, you can do this in April in an unheated greenhouse or polytunnel. Pot up your tubers in pots or crates in regular potting compost, give them a light watering and wait. Tubers can start into growth in as little as seven days but can take a lot longer.

On sunny, mild days plants can be moved outside to ensure new growth is hardened off. If a particularly cold night is forecast plants can be covered with fleece for a little extra protection. Check daily for signs of pest damage. Plants can be planted out after the last frost.

When your tubers have started to shoot it is also an ideal opportunity to divide them if you want to, as you will be able to see clearly where the shoots are. It is a good idea to divide tubers.

Planting tubers outside

Dahlias are one of those tricky plants that like a lot of water but need a free draining soil. They also need a lot of Sun. Being hungry plants they thrive in a rich soil and it is well worth spending some time before you are ready to plant adding some organic matter, such as well rotted manure, to your bed to improve the structure and fertility of the soil. To put it simply, dahlias are demanding divas and want the best of everything. They are also expensive and time consuming to grow, so its well worth trying to site them in the best and sunniest area of your plot.

Whether you have chosen to start your tubers early or not they can be planted outside when there is no longer a risk of frost. If you do get a frost forecast after planting any new growth can be protected using fleece. If an unforecast late frost blackens new growth, do not worry, the plant will usually just throw out new shoots a week or so later.

Tubers need to be planted so the tops of the tubers are 10 cm below the surface. The addition of a little bonemeal to the bottom of the planting hole will help the roots of the plants establish quickly.

Tubers should have a spacing of 60cm between them, although 90cm may be necessary for some of the giant varieties. If you do not already have permanent support posts in, it is best to put canes or posts in to act as supports before or at the time of planting. Trying to add stakes around established plants will mean that you can damage the roots.

If the soil is very dry water plants to help them establish. Remember to label plants as you go.

"There is nothing like the first hot days of spring when the gardener stops wondering if it's too soon to plant the dahlias and starts wondering if it's too late." – Henry Mitchell

Labelling plants

There is nothing more frustrating than getting to the end of the season and realising that the labels on your plants are illegible or missing. If you only grow a few varieties, it is worth investing in some very large durable labels, which are easy to see.

We have tried many ways of labelling over the years and have found many ways that just don't work. Permanent markers, even named brands, fade in the sun. Pencil is better but rubs off easily if your label is dirty or wet and you try to clean it. A chinagraph pencil is very durable, but difficult to write clearly with. Loop tie labels (the sort you get on trees in the garden centre) get brittle and break off after a season outside.

The best way we have found is to use a dymo labelling machine. This is time consuming and costly, but we have labels on dahlias that have been there for three years and still the printing is bold and clear. We print the variety names off and then stick them to oversized yellow plant labels cut from plastic sheets. The plastic is tough and durable, and the yellow colour means we can see them clearly. Each label gets hole punched at one end and can then be tied to the plant or the support cane. At the end of the season the label is then just tied to the tuber when it is lifted for storage.

Some dahlias have long names – so we use initials of varieties if it makes sense to us. JP is Josudi Polaris, WEJ is Wine Eyed Jill and ZMF is – well I'll leave you to work that one out.

Every year we still plant tubers or cuttings which have lost their label in our dedicated lost label bed. Every year we tell ourselves that when these plants flower we will identify and label them properly. Every October we act surprised when we get a frost and the flowers blacken and we can no longer identify the lost label plants. Next year I plan to leave labels and a pencil in a bag at the end of the row so we've no excuses.

Staking plants

Dahlias get tall, have heavy blooms and have thick brittle stems prone to breaking off at the base. The wind is your enemy, so siting your dahlias in a sunny position behind a windbreak, such as a hedge or a wall if you have one is a great idea. If you don't have a pre-existing windbreak, one can be created using builders debris netting or similar, hung between canes to dissipate the wind blowing across your dahlia rows. On a very open site try to plant your rows, so that the wind blows along them rather than across them.

Staking and supporting dahlias as they grow is essential. If you have a just a few you can do this by making a tripod of canes or hazel stakes around the base of the plant and using twine to tie stems in as they grow.

If you grow a lot of plants in dedicated dahlia beds, then you will perhaps want to look at something a little more efficient. Fenceposts or similar sturdy supports driven into the ground every 5m or so along your rows can be used to support a 15 cm mesh through which your plants can grow. You could use plastic mesh, more sustainable, but more costly cord mesh or, like we do, fencing wire usually used for keeping sheep in. In our set up, we have a pulley system which we can use to move the wire upwards as the dahlias grow taller.

This provides excellent support for the growing plants, but is expensive, needs some heft to install and is pretty permanent when you have it, so if you do need to move your dahlias to a new plot it is an added complication. We have moved our dahlias to a new plot, due to an unfortunate aminopyralid contamination (see problems, pests and diseases). We chose to leave the old frameworks in place and build new ones as it was easier to do so. The old framework is still very useful, albeit in an overkill kind of way, for growing cosmos, helichrysum and other tall annuals.

Young dahlia plants being planted below the support mesh.

Manipulating the size of flowers and timing blooming

People that grow for the show bench have a difficult task. They need to produce perfectly shaped blooms, of the correct size (yes, they have sets of rings to put over blooms to check!) And the blooms have to be at the perfect stage of opening on the day of the show. There are many techniques the exhibition growers use to help them achieve this. Cut flower growers will not need to worry about most of these things, but it is still good to have a little knowledge of the

Growing six up (or six straight up)

If you spend any time talking to growers who exhibit, you'll probably hear something like 'that variety is best grown six up'. All this means is that the variety makes the best sized blooms for exhibition if six lateral stems (the sideshoots that grow when the plant is stopped by removing the tip) are allowed to develop and bear flowers.

To get the right number of stems growers may have to 'double stop' – pinch out the growing tip again on a young lateral stem to create extra stems or 'strip down' - remove excess stems, usually stems which are weaker or excessively thick, to reduce the number of stems.

Stopping and thinning dahlias

Stopping a dahlia is the same as pinching out the tip of a stem.

For the cut flower grower, the main aim is to get the maximum amount of good quality blooms, pinching off the growing tips in June encourage side shoots to form, and every side shoot will produce flowers. More side shoots give more flowers. However, the more side shoots you allow to develop, the smaller the size of the blooms will be.

If we are not exhibiting, then there is no strict requirement that blooms are a certain size. All we need are plentiful, good quality blooms that are an easy size to work with, and we usually want those flowers to be ready as early in the season as possible. Every time a stem is 'stopped' the time to flowering is delayed a little. Ideally, we would like a good bushy plant to develop from a single stop. If after stopping plants, very few laterals develop then we could choose to stop again to create more stems.

For the exhibitor stopping times and thinning the amount of stems you allow to grow and bear flowers is a real art. By carefully planning when and how the dahlia plants are stopped, exhibitors can time when they will get their blooms and control the size of the bloom so that it meets show bench criteria.

Between planting and flowering

Plants will grow quickly. Slugs love dahlias so you will almost certainly have to use a method to control them, there are many things to try, from beer traps to slug pellets. How you manage pests will depend on your viewpoint on the use of poisons or artificial chemicals on your plot. Keep the rows weeded and water in dry spells. At the end of June plants should be tall and lush and as the dry season approaches it is beneficial to add a layer of mulch to the bed underneath your plants to keep down any persistent weeds and help with moisture retention but try to keep the bottom of stems clear. Water well before applying your mulch, you can use spent mushroom compost, well-rotted manure, straw or a mix of materials.

Keep a regular check on new shoots and buds and the underside of leaves for signs of damage by pests or disease. If spotted and dealt with early many problems can be tackled before they become major issues (see section on problems, pests and diseases).

Feeding

If you have used well-rotted manure or other nitrogen rich organic matter in your beds you will not need to feed your plants before they start to produce flowers. However, if your soil is deficient or leaches nutrients quickly you may wish to give a nitrogen rich feed, such as Chempak 2 early in the summer and then move on to a more balanced general-purpose feed as the season progresses.

When buds and flowers start to form switching to a lower nitrogen, higher potash feed such as tomato feed will promote good blooming.

When buds and flowers form

Continue to water and feed with tomato food. Watering should be done in the cooler parts of the day, preferably using drip irrigation or with a lance at the base of plants.

Disbudding

We regard disbudding of our dahlias as an essential task to ensure we get the best quality blooms on the longest, straightest stems possible. When the flower buds form at the top of stems they form in clusters of (usually) three buds. To disbud a stem is to remove the two side buds and leave just the one central bud to develop. At the same time work your way down the stem, removing the side shoots (laterals) and buds that have formed at the nodes beneath further down the stem. If possible, remove the laterals from both the second and third nodes on each stem.

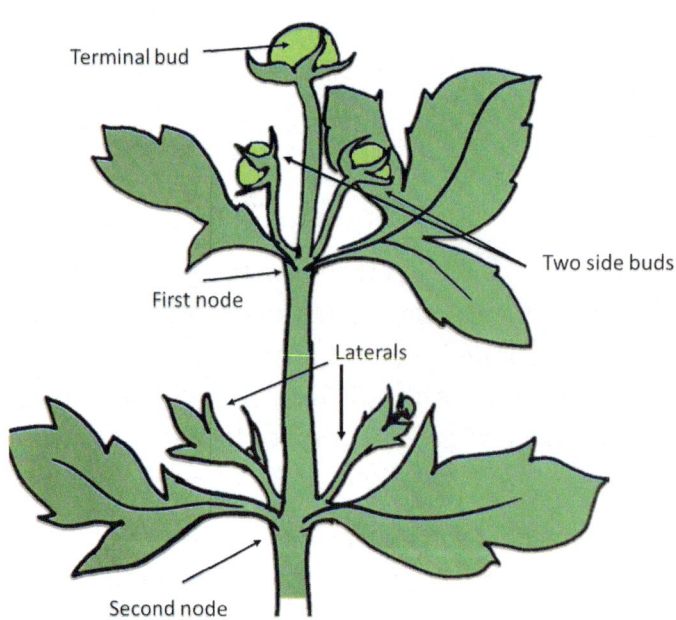

Terminal bud

Two side buds

First node

Laterals

Second node

Doing this focuses the energy into the one remaining bloom, which will be larger and show better form, facing upright upon a strong, straight stem.

It is time consuming, but we do try to disbud all of our dahlias, except for pompoms (where we are looking for smaller sized blooms) at least once weekly.

Damaged buds

Caterpillars or earwigs can nibble at buds and flowers, spoiling your hard work at the last hurdle. Caterpillars can be removed by hand when you see them, and earwig traps can be used to remove earwigs from the plot (see problems, pests and diseases).

If the terminal bud has been damaged, either by a pest or weather, simply remove it and leave one of the side buds to develop instead.

When will your dahlia bloom open?

One of the trickiest questions to answer when you grow cut flowers for a living is 'Will you have 50 stems of something or other in two weeks' time?' Exhibitors are very used to having to have their blooms perfectly open on the day of a show and so are very good judges of how long it will take the newly formed buds to open fully. Of course, this is just a guide and will vary a little depending on weather conditions and variety.

The following information is courtesy of John Thiermann from the Milwaukee area of the USA, who originally compiled the data. It was then distributed by the Southtown Dahlia Club.

http://www.southtowndahliaclub.com/

Terms used in the chart to describe buds –

Involucral bracts: Greenleaf like growth surrounding the emerging buds.

Baby bud: A tiny bud fully enclosed in the involucral bracts.

Pea bud: A bud that can be seen when the involucral bracts have opened.

Condition of terminal bud.	Days to Maturity
Baby bud visible within true leaves, which are more or less upright.	22-26 days
Baby bud emerging from, or just free of, true leaves.	20-22 days
Baby bud enlarged, but still entirely covered by bracts.	17-19 days
Small pea bud visible within bracts.	16-18 days

Big pea bud partly covered by bracts.	13-16 days
Bracts upright, but still touching at bud sides.	11-16 days
Bracts beginning to open out flat or are flat.	10-11 days
Tinge of colour visible, or petals loosening at centre.	7-9 days
Coloured petals loosening at centre.	6-7 days
1 – 5 petals lifting up straight.	6 days
Several petals upright or at 45 degrees, or some flat.	5 days
Petals upright or outer row of petals flat.	4 days
Nearly open or half open or some petals flat.	3 days
Almost fully open.	2 days
Fully open.	1 day
Mature.	

Green shading in the table shows the best time for cutting blooms for general sales.

Harvesting your blooms

Always try to cut your blooms in a cool part of the day, when the Sun is not so strong, preferably first thing in the morning.

If dahlias are cut while still in bud they will not open, if they are cut when fully open their vase life will only be two or three days. Therefore, unless you need a fully open bloom for an event, it is best to cut blooms from when they have started to unfurl their petals at about a third to halfway open.

Cut your stems long above a node, to promote new sideshoots to form.

Dahlias are thirsty flowers and after having lower foliage stripped, they should be quickly placed into a bucket of deep cool clean water for a long drink. The buckets of blooms should be left to condition in a cool, dark area for a few hours before bunching.

If selling just dahlias to a florist wrap gently in bunches of five or ten (depending on bloom size) in brown paper to protect the delicate blooms for transport.

While cutting make sure you also remove any spent flowers (unless you intend to collect seed) to focus the plant's energy back into producing more flowers.

Drying dahlias

Most dahlias dry very well and if hung up in a dark airy place where they will dry quickly, they keep their colour very well. Cut blooms for drying as soon as they are almost fully open.

Philippa Stewart of Just Dahlias is the expert at drying dahlia blooms in the UK.

Selling your blooms to florists

Dahlias are delicate flowers, and many do not have the longest vase life. Experienced florists will know this, but it is important that you manage the expectations of new florist customers. We have become so used to lacklustre bunches of flowers from the import market. Mass produced chrysanthemum, carnation, and roses, often dipped in chemicals to prolong their vase life make them easy and economical for the florist to work with. But they do not have the sparkle and pazzaz of a freshly cut dahlia. So, for the florist it is a trade-off. They need to adapt their practice to use dahlias well. But using dahlias will give their bouquets and floristry work that extra special hand-curated look, that will be eye catching and original. And by using seasonal, locally grown blooms the florist will be working more sustainably, while supporting the local economy. If a florist does choose to use locally grown dahlias in their work always cut as fresh as you can and give them only the highest quality blooms. Setting them up to succeed, will earn you a return customer, promote British grown and ultimately help all British growers.

Availability is also an issue that needs to be explained clearly to customers. Dahlias are available only in the summer months, from July until the first frost. Even experienced florists still ask us what our chances are of having dahlias for events in late June or late October. Never guarantee the dates you will have blooms ready. Instead ask florists to focus on the wonderful seasonality of them and to offer their clients a suitable alternative focal flower as a back-up. For early summer, this could be garden roses, or for autumn, bloom chrysanthemums.

Selling dahlias in retail bunches

We sell hundreds of mixed retail bunches every week. These are smaller sized bunches, that our customers buy, usually for themselves, to pop in a vase on their kitchen table at home. Our customers usually buy a bunch once a week. If we are including dahlias is these bunches, we only use the smaller headed ball, pompon, or waterlily blooms. If is important to use only dahlias that have been freshly cut and conditioned well to ensure they are fully hydrated, so that they will give our customers the vase life they expect.

Promote dahlias as a seasonal treasure, much like peonies in early summer. A short-lived luxury, only with us for a limited time and make them desirable. Mix them with flowers that have a longer vase life, such as statice, achillea, grasses and amaranthus. That way your customer will be able to remove faded blooms, and still have flowers looking good at the end of the week.

At the height of the season when you may have excess blooms, which you will need to cut to prolong flowering, you could sell bunches of just five or seven colour themed dahlias wrapped in brown paper. Run a social media promotion and they will fly out like the proverbial hot cakes.

Above all it is vital to practice good stock rotation. We have a two-day rule. Any bunch that has not sold on the second day is taken off sale. If it's particularly hot, then we move that down to one day. Our mixed bunches contain a high proportion of flowers that are suitable for drying, after two days these are still in perfect condition, so off sale does not mean a loss. We just pull out any blooms that do not dry well and hang the rest of the bunch upside down in a dry, dark and airy space to create mini dried bouquets.

Typical mixed bunches with dahlias for the retail market

Using dahlias in event work

Dahlias make spectacular flowers for events. They lend themselves so well to creating archways, urns and opulent table centrepieces. Unlike other flowers they come in a huge range of sizes from a 4 or 5 cm across to the 30 cm giants and a vast array of colours, so there are dahlias that are suitable for every aspect of event floristry.

For thirsty flowers, dahlias last surprisingly well out of water, especially the varieties with a tight formation and high petal count. This makes them ideal for wedding bouquets and buttonholes. Just ensure they are fully hydrated before use.

Lauren's wedding flowers used dark Rip City and La Recoleta dahlias to contrast with peach roses. Photo courtesy of Tara Gillen Photography. The Dahlia symbolizes eternal bonds of commitment, so it is a popular flower choice for weddings.

For pedestals, table decoration, arches and urns, chicken wire frameworks, stuffed with wet moss will help your dahlias stay looking fresh all day.

However, if they are to be used in an outdoor location, especially if it is breezy and warm, varieties which have loose, large petals will start to look tired quite quickly. If possible, place larger blooms into water containers that can be pushed into a chicken wire framework and secured in place with twine or re-usable zip ties. Your water containers could be flower tubes, grave vases or simply water bottles with the tops cut off. Any visible mechanics can be wrapped in moss to cover them.

Seed saving and hybridising

If you do decide you would like to have a go at hybridising dahlias, there are a few things you can do to try and maximise the chances of getting some progeny that are worth keeping. Dahlia breeders raise new varieties from seed all the time. However, in the past the main aim of dahlia hybridizing was to produce a plant that was either fantastic for the show bench or very saleable for garden use. The suitability of flowers for cutting has always been a secondary consideration. But now the resurgence in popularity of the dahlia as a cut flower, coupled with the growth of small-scale growers who are always seeking new varieties to grow, has meant that new hybrids, bred specifically for the cut flower trade are being created.

It is not an easy task, the dominant genetic traits in dahlias are not the traits we, as cut flower growers, would like to see. The dominant genes will control the appearance of the offspring. And with dahlias the dominant genes code for flowers with a single row of petals with an open centre which face downwards on long, weak stems. As cut flower growers we want double blooms, with no yellow centre showing which are facing upwards atop strong, straight stems. Basically, the exact opposite.

In the British climate the growing season is relatively short, viable pollen is only produced in warm weather and the risk of rain rotting seedheads before they are ripe is high, so if you wish to raise your own seeds to save, then do start as early in the season as you can.

Open and selective pollination

Open pollination is when you let nature take its course and allow insects to pollinate the dahlias on your plot. The seeds collected may well produce some lovely flowers, but they will almost always be open centred with a low petal count.

Of course, if you grow only the highest quality plants and remove any which show a tendency to weak stems or open centred flowers, your chances of producing useful offspring are much improved.

You can further increase your chances of getting the dahlia offspring you would like by growing only a limited variety of dahlias in blocks away from all other varieties.

Hand pollination

Dahlias are not the easiest blooms to pollinate. They are composite flowers made up of lots of individual flowers grouped together to give the appearance of one bloom. Each flower within the composite will produce just one seed, and to do this each one must be pollinated separately. However, if you are successful, hand-pollination does allow you to be sure of which your parent plants are. Self-pollination is also an option, where pollinating a bloom with its own pollen can result in offspring, which will be different to the parent plant but may have worthwhile characteristics.

Parts of a dahlia flower

Composite Inflorescence

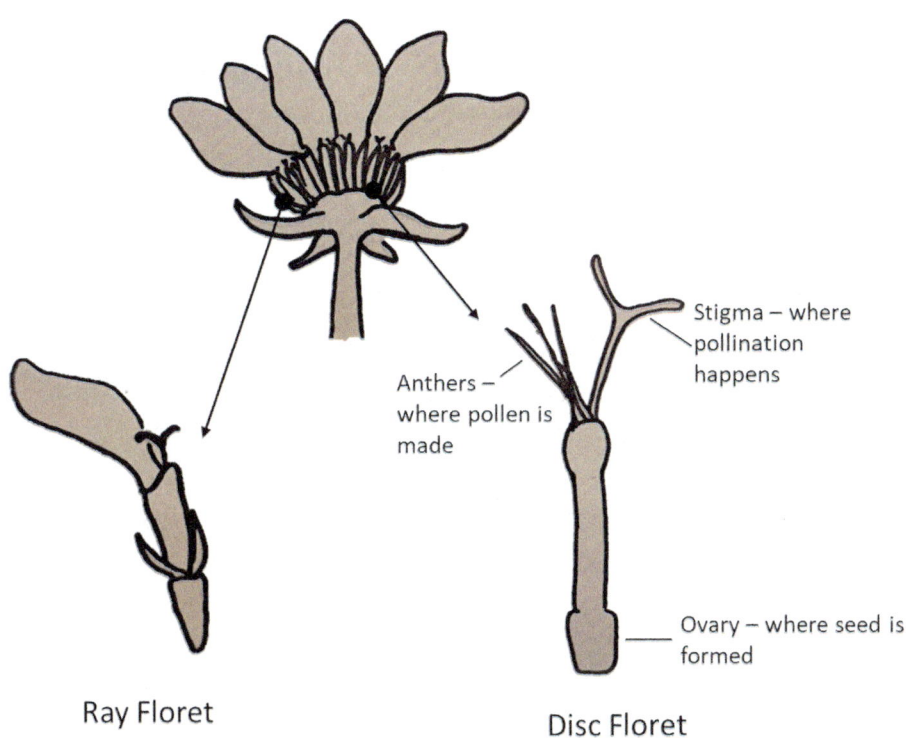

Stigma – where pollination happens

Anthers – where pollen is made

Ovary – where seed is formed

Ray Floret

Disc Floret

Individual Inflorescence

Step 1 - Selecting parent plants.

Select only plants that you know to be excellent, in the colours and shapes you are interested in breeding. They should be healthy, vigorous growers, that make good tubers.

Step 2 – prevent insect pollination.

Cover new flower buds with organza bags to stop insects reaching the blooms and allow the flowers to develop inside the bags.

Step 3 – collect the pollen.

When the flowers are fully open you should see the centre disc. Some petals may start to fall, so you should remove these from the bag. In the British climate it is advantageous at this stage to carefully hand remove a lot of the petals to get rid of moisture and minimise the risk of the centre of your dahlia rotting. When you start to see pollen on the anthers you can try to collect it. You'll need to do this on a dry, still day. Hold a piece of paper, or paper bag (I use a paper cupcake case) underneath the flower and tap the flower to see if pollen falls onto the paper. You can also use a small paintbrush to gently brush pollen onto the paper. If the pollen does not want to fall it is probably not ready yet, or a little damp, so pop the bag back on it and try again the next day. You can collect pollen every day from your bloom until it stops producing.

The pollen can be sealed in a paper bag or cone and kept somewhere dry for a couple of days if you are not ready to use it straight away.

Step 4 – hand pollination.

When the stigma on the flower head is ready it will have opened up to make a 'y' shape and you should be able to use your small brush to transfer the pollen you have collected to the surface of the stigma where it should now stick. The now (hopefully pollinated flower head) should be sealed once more inside the organza bag. It is a good idea to revisit the flower with extra pollen from your chosen pollen parent every day for about three days to increase the chances of successful pollination.

Step 5 – wait.

Now you simply need to wait with the seed head firmly sealed in its organza bag until it is ripe. The main problem now will be moisture. Rain, dew and colder mornings can cause the seed head to rot before the seeds ripen. The seedhead will take around six weeks to mature, during this time, it will become elongated and conical in shape. If there is a period of prolonged rain forecast and your seedheads are nearing maturity, then you may be better off cutting them and bring them into the house. If you pop them in a vase in a bright airy place they will continue to mature and may still produce seed.

Step 6 – collect your seed.

After about six weeks you can gently peel back the outer layer of bracts on your seedhead to see if the seeds (if they are present!) are ready. If they are green they are not. If they are black, they are. The bracts should be dry and papery. Once the seeds are ready simply separate them out from the rest of the seedhead and store them in little paper envelopes, as you would any other seed in a cool, dry, and dark place until you are ready to sow them in spring.

Problems, pests and diseases

Problems

Mineral deficiencies

The composition and pH of your soil will have an effect on the availability of minerals for healthy growth. A healthy soil with a crumbly texture, rich in organic matter is ideal, as it allows for minerals to be transported easily into the roots of the plants. Dahlias thrive in a soil which is neutral or slightly acidic pH 6.5 is ideal.

If the leaves on your dahlia plants look yellow, it is very possible that mineral deficiency is the problem.

Magnesium deficiency – yellowing on older leaves.

Iron deficiency (less common) – yellowing on younger leaves rather than old leaves.

High potassium levels can affect the uptake of other minerals so if a deficiency is evident and you are feeding with a potassium rich feed you should discontinue this for a while.

Herbicide contamination

In the UK we have seen a recent rise in cases of herbicide contamination in composts and farmyard manure. In particular aminopyralids, which are used to control broad-leaved weeds in grass crops have found their way into commercially prepared composts and manures where they can persist for several years. Their effect on a bed of dahlias can be devastating. Plants which are exposed to these herbicides will show stunted growth and deformations. New growth will appear twisted and curled.

Prevention is better than cure and if you have bought in soil, compost or manure and you are unsure of its provenance it may be wise to check by using it to grow some tomatoes or beans, before you use it on the rest of your plot. If they grow normally, it is a good indication that your compost is safe to use.

If you suspect that you have a herbicide contamination in your beds (and have double checked to rule out thrip or spider mite infestation) then there is no quick fix and you may lose plants. Over time, as it rains, the herbicides will leach from the soil naturally so watering regularly will speed up this process. If you can get rid of the contaminants in time you should be able to save your plants, although they will be weakened.

Challenging weather conditions

Late or early frosts – we've all been caught out by an unexpected frost. Dahlias are much more resilient than people give them credit for. If your dahlia leaves get blackened by a one-off frost, simply cut your plants back to remove the damaged growth and they will soon put on new healthy growth.

Excessive rain – once established, dahlias usually cope well with wet conditions, although flower buds may suffer from botrytis in extended periods of dull, wet weather. However, if your plants start to look like they are wilting, even though the soil is wet, it is a sign that the stem bases or tubers may have rotted. Newly planted tubers will not like sitting in wet soil for long, so if your soil does not drain well and excessive rainfall has caused flooding some tubers may rot before they start to grow.

Excessive heat – Dahlias usually cope well with hot weather, especially if you can get out early to water them regularly, before the Sun is up. However, in really hot conditions the quality of the blooms can be compromised. Colours can be bleached or change to more yellow tones and more blooms can become 'daisy eyed' - where the centre is open and showing the yellow stamens. The plants will usually recover well and start producing better blooms when the weather cools dawn again.

Drought – dahlias will not grow well and not flower if they do not have sufficient water. If you have a lot of dahlias drip irrigation and applying a layer of mulch in early Summer will make it easier to ensure your dahlias are well watered in drought conditions.

Pests

<u>Slugs and snails</u> can quickly demolish all of the new growth on dahlia plants. There are numerous ways to try to control the numbers of slugs and snails in your dahlia beds.

- Surrounding the base of plants with a ring of copper forms a barrier which slugs and snails do not like to cross.

- Surrounding plants with crushed eggshells, grit, cat litter or other gritty material.

- Beer traps sunk into the soil.

- Slug pellets. Iron (III) phosphate pellets are more traditional but newer products are being developed such as sheep wool pellets.

<u>Aphids, thrips and spider mites</u> can all cause yellowing of leaves and distorted growth and like all sap feeding pests, they can transmit viruses from one plant to another, so it is very important that you act quickly to control their numbers.

For aphid infestations in an enclosed area, biological controls such as lacewing and ladybird larvae can be used.

In larger outdoor beds natural predators should already be present and their numbers will increase as the number of aphids do.

Spraying with a non-chemical based pest control such as SB plant invigorator can be effective, as can spraying plants with a strong jet of water from a hosepipe. This treatment will be effective for aphids, thrips and spider mite.

Aphids and thrips are usually fairly easy to spot. However, spider mites are tiny and difficult to see. You may see small orange dots on the underside of affected leaves, but it is easier to spot the webs they make.

In hot, dry years spider mite infestations can be very damaging and spread quickly. Spraying the underside of leaves with water can be effective in reducing their numbers as they cannot survive in very wet conditions. Badly damaged leaves with infestations of mites can be removed and burned.

Earwigs love to eat dahlias making holes in both buds and leaves. Simple earwig traps can be very effective. Place an upside-down flowerpot stuffed with straw on top of a cane. Earwigs will gather in the straw, which you can then remove and dispose of, along with the earwigs, as you see fit.

Diseases

Powdery mildew in warm, wet years powdery mildew may be a problem, although it is rarely serious it can cause unsightly discolouration with leaves looking white and dusty.

Verticillum Wilt is a fungal disease which causes the collapse of the vessels that carry water through the stems and leaves of the plant. Affected plants will wilt and black streaks may be present on stems. There is no cure and affected plants should be removed and destroyed.

Leafy Gall and Crown Galls are caused by bacteria in the soil. With leafy gall you will see peculiar looking, dense clusters of shoots and leaves forming instead of the usual two or three shots you would usually expect to form at an eye. With crown gall a cauliflower like mass forms on the crown of the dahlia. Diseased tubers will perform poorly and get worse over time. As the disease is spread by bacteria in the soil it can be transferred to other plants nearby. Diseased tubers should be dug up and destroyed, soil in beds where they have been grown should be replaced and the tools which have come into contact with the diseased tubers should be disinfected.

Viruses – dahlia mosaic virus, spotted wilt virus

Look out for patchy yellowing of leaves, yellow streaks along stems and veins of leaves, stunted or deformed growth and deformations of bud and flowers. Viruses usually come from unwittingly importing infected stock. The virus can then be spread by aphids to healthy plants.

A dahlia leaf showing yellow blotches, particularly along veins (known as vein clearing), due to virus.

Unfortunately, many symptoms of virus infection in dahlias are easily confused with insect infestation damage, or nutrient deficiencies. If you suspect you have a dahlia virus, you may wish to check in one of the many online dahlia growing forums.

There is no treatment for the viruses that affect dahlias, so infected plants should be destroyed and any tools that have come into contact with infected plants should be sterilized.

Overwintering your tubers. To lift or not to lift?

In many areas of the UK there may not be a choice about whether to lift your dahlias or not. If your soil is heavy, lays wet in the winter, or you live in an area which experiences very cold winters, then you will need to lift your dahlia tubers and store them somewhere, dry, dark and frost free for the winter period.

However, in milder areas if you have a light, freely draining soil you will probably be safely able to leave them in the ground all year round. A layer of mulch over the top of dormant plants can be used protect tubers from very cold weather.

Aside from helping your tubers to survive the colder months, there are other reasons to lift your plants in late Autumn or early Winter. Lifting tubers enables you to split them into more manageable sized plants and increase your stock. It provides you with the opportunity to wake some of your tubers up early in the Spring and take cuttings and it can help you to spot early signs of disease, such as galls.

The majority of plants in the beds here are raised from cuttings. This ensures our stock is as healthy as it can be, with flowers that are of the best quality and colour. In August or September, we mark the plants which we want to use to take cuttings from the next year, choosing only the healthiest which have flowers showing the best form and colour. When we lift them, these tubers go into a crate which we store separately as we will retrieve this one first, in February, to begin the process of waking up the selected parent tubers to take our cuttings for the coming year.

When to lift

If you are lifting, you can do this anytime from late October. You do not need to wait for a killing frost to blacken the leaves but most growers do, as the longer the dahlia has to store energy in its tuber, the more likely it is that the tuber will make it through the winter.

Dahlias in the field, blackened from an early frost.

If you, like us, are on cold wet clay and have a lot to lift, you may wish to start early before the inevitable wet weather sets in.

As long as you have got your dahlias lifted before the really deep ground frosts begin (usually in late December or January in our area) the tubers should be fine.

How to lift and dry tubers

Cut back foliage, dig carefully around the base of the plant to loosen the soil and assess the size and depth of the tuber. Get a broad fork underneath the tuber and use it to lift the dahlia from the ground. Try to avoid pulling the dahlia up by the stem, as the stems will easily snap off at the neck and the neck is where the new shoots will form for next year's growth.

Newly lifted dahlia tubers ready for drying.

When you have lifted your dahlia, you will need to set it to dry. Gently remove any excess dirt, label your dahlia and turn it upside down on a rack somewhere dry and frost free. Placing the tubers upside down allows excess water to drain out of the hollow stems. Although drying space is always at a premium try not to overcrowd the tubers in your drying space as they will dry more quickly if spaced out, and be less likely to rot.

Some growers wash their tubers to remove every bit of dirt before storing them. We do not, it is difficult enough getting them dry in the first place without giving them a soaking with the hose as well. However, cleaning them does make it easier to see the condition of the tubers and split them if you choose to do so.

How long you dry your dahlias for depends on the weather conditions. The best time to box up your dahlias is when the tubers feel dry to the touch but while they are still fat, and firm.

If you wish to you could split your tubers, into smaller more manageable pieces before storing. This increases your stock and makes them easier to store. When splitting tubers, you must ensure that each smaller piece has at least one tuber, a section of neck and at least one eye. The eyes can be quite difficult to see if the tuber is dormant so many growers choose not to divide their stock until Spring when the dahlia starts to wake up and the eyes are more visible.

How to store your tubers

Tubers can be packed into boxes or crates surrounded by straw, paper, or wood chippings (but beware, as mice will think this is a lovely winter home and the tubers will provide them with lovely meals over the winter months.)

They can also be stored in dry compost or vermiculite in storage crates. Smaller tubers can be wrapped in clingfilm, to stop them becoming desiccated and packed side by side into boxes.

Once packed your boxes or crates should be kept somewhere frost free and dry and inspected at regular intervals to ensure none have started to rot.

If you notice some of your dahlias have signs of rot on them (soft tubers which are seeping and have a distinctive unpleasant smell) you can trim them up and cut away any rotten portions to stop the rot spreading. A dusting of any cut surfaces with sulfur or cinnamon will help sterilise and seal any wounds.

Choosing varieties that make good cut flowers

Dahlias are classified into groups by their flower shapes and then again by sizes. It is a complex system used mainly for defining exhibition classes. Discussions about which group some dahlias fit into are frequent as the differences between some groups or size ranges are slight.

A simplified description of the groups is given below.

Group 1 – Single dahlias. A single outer row of petals surrounding a central disc.

Group 2 – Anemone-flowered dahlias. Outer rows of petals surround a cluster of ray shaped florets.

Group 3 – Collarette dahlias. An outer row of petals surrounds an inner ring of smaller petals around the central disc.

Group 4 – Waterlily dahlias. Cupped petals open out into a bloom resembling a waterlily in shape.

Group 5 – Decorative dahlias. Fully double blooms with no central disc.

Group 6 - Ball dahlias. Fully double blooms, ball shaped.

Group 7 – Pompon dahlias. Fully double, small ball shaped blooms.

Group 8 – Cactus dahlias. Fully double blooms with pointed petals.

Group 9 – Semi-cactus dahlias. Fully double blooms, with pointed petals, which are broader at the base than those of cactus dahlias.

Group 10 - All the dahlias that don't fit into another group, including the species dahlias.

Group 11 – Fimbriated dahlias. Petals are split at the ends, giving the flowers a frilly appearance.

Group 12 – Star dahlias. A single row of petals, curled to a point, surround a central disc.

Group 13 – Double orchid dahlias. Double blooms with no central disc and a central triangular shaped petal formation.

Group 14 – Paeony dahlias. Have many rows of petals that surround a central disc.

Group 15 – Fully double blooms, with narrow reflexed petals, usually with a pointed tip.

Some of the groups are further split into miniature, small, medium or giant according to the size of their flowers.

Miniature Flowered -

These cultivars have blooms usually not exceeding 10 cm (4.ins) in diameter.

Small Flowered -

These cultivars have blooms usually between 10 cm (4ins) and 15 cm (6ins).

Medium Flowered -

These cultivars have blooms usually between 15 cm (6ins) and 20 cm (8ins).

Large Flowered -

These cultivars have blooms usually between 20 cm (8ins) and 25 cm (10ins).

Giant Flowered -

These cultivars have blooms usually over 25 cm (10ins) in diameter.

-

The best types of dahlias to grow for cut flowers are from the ball, pompom, waterlily and decorative groups. Some cactus, semi cactus, anemone flowered and stellar dahlias also have good cutting qualities.

In general, the tighter the petal formation and the more petals a dahlia flower has, the better it's vase life.

Giant decorative dahlias, like the ever-popular Café au Lait, do not have a good vase life, giving three days at best, and are too big to work well in retail bouquets. However due to their colouration and blousy appearance they are always in demand for weddings and events. If you supply weddings you will want to grow them.

(Please note that dahlias varieties which are available in the USA, Australia or New Zealand are not always available here, so it is better to use British resources to help you if creating a dahlia wish list and avoid the disappointment of lusting after an American dahlia variety, which is impossible to source here.)

Helpfully some suppliers use a code letter to tell you which dahlias are suited for a particular purpose. G – Garden, C – Cut Flower, E – Exhibition, P – Pot or Patio.

In the following pages I have included a list of our favourite varieties of dahlias that we have found good for cutting or for event work. But of course, there are so many varieties of dahlias to choose from, with more very good ones being bred every year, that even the most avid collector cannot trial them all! You will notice a lot of pompon types in our list. We make up a lot of smaller and medium sized bouquets for the retail trade, and the size and vase life of the pompons suits this purpose very well. So, when choosing the dahlias you would like to grow, do consider how the blooms will be used.

Our favourite varieties (so far!)

White

Josudi Polaris

Miniature cactus. Long stems bear white flowers. Prolific and useful.

Kenora Challenger

A large semi-cactus white dahlia, popular with exhibitors. Stunning.

L'Ancress

Ball dahlia. An old but much-loved variety, which produces consistent and perfect, white blooms, occasionally flushed with lilac at the centres.

Ryecroft Brenda T

A lovely small decorative dahlia. White with a hint of pinky lavender at the centre. Very healthy and perfect for wedding work.

White Ballerina

A stunning pure white waterlily dahlia. Blooms are well formed, on top of long, straight stems.

White Aster

Large Pompon. Prolific, dainty white blooms which are perfect for wedding work and buttonholes.

Cream

Café Au Lait

Giant decorative blooms, of variable colour, from softest pink to the milky coffee it is named for. Much in demand for wedding work. Like all giant decorative the blooms have a short vase life of three days.

Cameo

A beautifully coloured waterlily dahlia with ivory flowers. Very good stem lengths and prolific. However, early in the season the petals are easily discoloured by rain or insect damage.

Sweet Nathalie

A small decorative dahlia with colours just like Café Au Lait, which makes it very useful.

Pink

Arbatax

A decorative dahlia with white petals edged with pink.

Bracken Ballerina

A delicate and elegant waterlily dahlia, with palest pink blooms on long stems. Healthy and free flowering.

Dikara Superb

A lovely mid pink decorative dahlia. Superb as the name suggests, with long stems ideal for cutting.

Evannah

A decorative dahlia with medium sized blooms. Loose heads of variably coloured pink and white petals.

Gerrie Hoek

Mid pink waterlily blooms, borne on long, straight stems.

Hamari Rose

Miniature ball with lovely pink flowers, prolific and very easy. Superb for cutting.

Rosemary's Blush

Beautiful Pompon with palest pink blooms, occasionally peachy. Lovely.

Salmon Runner

Bright salmon pink flowers prolifically produced on long, strong stems. Makes a very good cut flower.

Shiloh Noelle

A giant decorative with ruffled petals that are delicately blush coloured with a hint of lavender. A brilliant dahlia for wedding work.

Sweet Love

A pink and white decorative dahlia, with good strong straight stems, perfect for cutting. We were given one of these by a friend who had been sent it by a Dutch supplier instead of the Peaches variety she had ordered. However, it is a good one and well worth keeping.

Wizard of Oz

A very useful pale bink small ball dahlia, its size and delicate colour make it easy to work with.

Peach and Coral

Aljo

A strong growing semi cactus, with large salmon pink flowers, which are borne freely on long straight stems. Healthy and blends well with most other colours.

American Dawn

Beautiful coloured decorative dahlia, with peachy, orange outer petals and purple centre. Plants are strong growing with thick stems, which are very sturdy. The flower stems can tend to being a little on the short side, so water well and remove side shoots from flowering stems.

Burlesca

A very pretty small ball dahlia, with multicoloured petals of soft yellow flushed with coral and pink.

Carolina Wagemans

A lovely waterlily dahlia with blooms that vary from mid to pale peach depending on the weather. Long straight stems, and always in demand.

Jowey Winnie

Ball dahlia. Beautiful dusky coral-coloured flowers with a hint of lilac at the centres. Very much sought after by florists.

Labyrinth

A giant decorative mostly suitable for wedding or event work, due to its shorter vase life. Twisted petals are beautifully coloured in blends of peach, pink and coral.

Linda's baby

A very lovely peachy ball dahlia which always sells well.

Molly Raven

A lovely dark leaved decorative dahlia with petals ranging from apricot to pink to burgundy. Freely flowering with long, strong stems.

Palmares

Usefully coloured decorative dahlia, with good strong stems. Peach outer petals, which become more yellow as the season progresses, surround a deeper pink centre.

Peaches (in the US this is known as peaches and cream)

Always in demand this decorative dahlia has beautiful peach-coloured blooms and a lovely shape. Not to be confused with the peaches and cream sold in Europe which has a very different flower which has orangey yellow petals tipped with white.

Rosemary's Dawn

Perfect and prolific peachy orange pompon. A really useful colour and size.

Sweet Suzanne

A very prolific bloomer, Sweet Suzanne is a peachy coloured small decorative dahlia. The colour becomes tends to become more yellow later in the season or in hot weather.

Wine eyed Jill

A lovely peach ball dahlia with a deep pink centre. Good strong stems. The flowers become more yellow as the season progresses.

Zundert Mystery Fox

Glowing coral-coloured blooms on long, strong stems. A very eye-catching decorative dahlia. Healthy and easy.

Yellow

Caribbean Fantasy

An exotic-coloured decorative dahlia, with cream petals streaked with yellow, white and red. Healthy and freely blooming.

Hapet Compo

A very nice pompon dahlia with pale lemon petals that have a burgundy flush at the centre of the bloom. Healthy and strong, flowers freely and goes with everything.

Maya

A variable decorative dahlia of soft yellow with petals flushed pink. Goes with everything.

Orange

Brown Sugar

A beautiful ball dahlia, with intense coppery almost burnt sienna flowers. One of the richest coloured dahlias, great for Autumn floristry.

Cornel Brons

A very good ball dahlia, which is exceptionally healthy and produces masses of perfect mid orange blooms on long. straight stems. Prolific, makes good tubers and easy to propagate.

Irish Glow

The lovliest vibrant orange flowers, often just flushed with a touch of red. A very useful small pompon.

Jowey Linda
A strong bright orange ball dahlia, perfect for autumn work.

Kasagi

A pompon dahlia with bright yellow blooms edged with orange, very healthy and prolific.

Nicholas

A very nice orange water lily dahlia with long, straight stems, perfect for cutting.

Winkie Lambrusco

A very lovely bright orange pompon dahlia, with perfect form. Reliable.

Red

Chick a Dee

Pompon dahlia with variable red and white blooms. Each bloom shows a different colour variation, some are pure dark red, and some are highly mottled with white. Makes good tubers.

Red Jill

A good and productive bright red ball dahlia, with long strong stems.

Sheval Megan

A perfect red dahlia, strong and healthy. This small decorative has a strong unfading colour, good stems and great vase life.

Burgundy

Barbarry D'Amour

A beautiful burgundy miniature decorative with good strong stems.

Dark Spirit

A small ball dahlia with rich, burgundy-coloured blooms, flowers freely and gives lots of long stems for cutting.

Rip City

A perfect and productive burgundy decorative (classified by some as a semi cactus) dahlia. Uniform, medium sized blooms on long, strong stems. It's our favourite burgundy dahlia.

Purple and lilac

Aurwen's Violet

A useful rich purple pompom dahlia.

Crème de Cassis

A decorative dahlia with an unusual colouring of lilac petals with blackberry-coloured undersides. Its colour make this one of the dahlias we choose to grow, even though it is tricky to get a good length on the stems. Removing sideshoots on flowering stems essential to get enough length.

Downham Royal

Small ball blooms on long, straight stems. A very useful rich purple colour.

Rocco
A useful purple pompon dahlia with good long stems.

Genova

A very pretty small decorative dahlia with white and lilac blooms.

Josudi Andromeda

Miniature cactus. Long stems bear beautiful and delicate white and lilac Flowers, which make a lovely cut flower.

Noreen

A very beautiful pale lilac/ pink pompon dahlia. Perfect for buttonholes.

Willo's Violet

A very healthy and prolific mid violet pompom dahlia.

Notes

Dahlia wishlist (one page is never enough!)

Dahlia suppliers

These dahlia suppliers are UK based and most produce all, or some of their cuttings and tubers 'in-house'. This significantly decreases the chances of importing diseased tubers or receiving mislabelled varieties.

Halls of Heddon - https://www.hallsofheddon.com/

JR Gott - https://jrgdahlias.com/

Withypitt Dahlias - http://www.withypitts-dahlias.co.uk/

Woolmans - https://www.woolmans.com/

Where to see dahlias

Halls of Heddon dahlia fields

An amazing display of some of the best varieties available in the UK.

The dahlia field is open usually from the end of August until October, but check their website before planning a visit as exact opening dates vary depending from year to year.

Ayletts nursery

Ayletts nursery near St Albans have a dahlia field where you can see many varieties grown en-masse and a lovely herbaceous show garden where you can see dahlias grown as part of the mixed borders.

Gilberts Dahlias

A dahlia field attached to the nursery near Romsey in Hampshire. Many varieties on display, usually open from mid-August to October.

The National Dahlia Collection

The National Collection is in Cornwall and open to visitors on selected days throughout the season.

Shows and exhibitions

The Northern National Show (formerly Harrogate)

Wisely Show

Do check the National Dahlia Societies Website to find dahlia shows or exhibitions near you.

National Trust and private gardens

Anglesy Abbey

Ninety-eight acres of parkland and gardens, including a dahlia garden, near Cambridge.

Dyffryn

A fifty-five acre site on the outskirts of Cardiff including some lovely dahlia beds and mixed herbaceous planting.

Great Dixter

Christopher Lloyds famous garden near Rye in East Sussex. Mixed borders with lots of dahlias to enjoy.

Hyde Hall

An RHS garden in Chelmsford in Essex. Lovely herbaceous borders and traditional planting with many dahlias to enjoy.

Kelmarsh Hall

The gardens at Kelmarsh Hall in Northamptonshire include a large walled garden, in which a wide variety of dahlias are grown.

Mount Stewart

An RHS partner garden in Newtownards, County Down. Many beautiful plant combinations to see.

Rousham Gardens

A beautiful garden near Bicester in Oxfordshire, with a lovely selection of dahlias grown along the wall in the kitchen garden.

Valley Gardens

A seventeen acre public park in Harrogate with herbaceous borders, dahlia beds and traditional formal beds.

Wisley

The RHS flagship garden in Woking in Surrey. As well as traditional garden areas and glasshouses Wisley has a trials garden where you can see many different dahlia varieties.

Further reading

Dahlia Breeding for the Farmer-Florist and the Home Gardener – Kristine Albrecht

An excellent an in-depth guide to the world of breeding new dahlia varieties. A must if you want to further your knowledge of hybridising.

Dahlias – Ted Collins

A very good book with everything you need to know with an emphasis on exhibiting.

Connie's Dahlias a Beginners Guide – Connie Thompson

Excellent and informative – written for the Canadian / Northern American market. Although the climate and some of the pests and diseases will be different, the skills and techniques are the same worldwide.

Floret Farm's Discovering Dahlias – Erin Benzakein

Lots of lovely photos and inspiration. Written for the US market, so some featured varieties are not available for purchase in other countries.

Useful websites

The National Dahlia Society

https://www.dahlia-nds.co.uk/

Halls of Heddon

https://www.hallsofheddon.com/

JRG Dahlias

https://jrgdahlias.com/

Withypitt dahlias

https://withypitts-dahlias.co.uk/

Darren Everest Dahlias

http://www.darreneverestdahlias.co.uk/

Floret Farm

https://www.floretflowers.com/resources/how-to-grow-dahlias

Dahlia Virus ID

https://dahlia.org/wp-content/uploads/2018/01/ADS-DMV_Symptoms_Slides.pdf

Fun facts and interesting ideas

- Dahlias are the national flower of Mexico.

- The Aztecs used the hollow stems of the dahlia to transport water and the tubers as a food source.

  It is still used in Oaxacan cuisine. Dacopa is an extract from the roasted tubers, and is used to flavour drinks, which are a little like a mochaccino.

Dahlia rosti recipe (Inspired by James Wong)

Use larger, plump dahlia tubers. Preferably from the plant you bought for a pound on offer that turned out to be nothing like the plant you thought you were getting.

Peel and grate the tubers. Salt and set aside for half an hour and then squeeze to remove excess water.

Grate a small onion and mix with the grated dahlia tuber, along with one egg, a tablespoon of flour some nutmeg, pepper and any other herbs or spices you fancy (cumin, chilli flakes, paprika).

Fry tablespoons full in oil until golden brown.

Serve as a starter or snack with sour cream or sweet chilli dip or as a side with curries.

Different varieties of dahlias are said to have different flavours; however, we have only tried them once and the one we tried (variety unknown) tasted of nothing much at all.

- In the nineteenth century, a London newspaper offered £1 to the first breeder to create a blue dahlia—the reward has never been claimed.

- A fruit sugar called inulin which is extracted from dahlia tubers. This was used to make a substance called Atlantic starch or diabetic sugar. Atlantic Starch was used to treat diabetes (and consumption) until the discovery of insulin in 1923.

  Inulin is still used in kidney function tests.

- Around 840 babies are given the name Dahlia every year.

- The tree dahlia, *Dahlia imperialis*, can grow to 3m in height in a single year. It has beautiful pink single flowers, but it is very difficult to get it to flowering size in the UK. If you like a challenge this is the one for you.

Acknowledgements

Firstly thanks to my father and Jack's grandfather, Michael for inspiring us to not only grow dahlias, but to strive to do it to the best of our ability.

Many thanks to the knowledgeable members of the National Dahlia Society, who share their knowledge so freely, so that others may learn.

Printed in Great Britain
by Amazon